COMING OUT PARTY

WORDS BY

REBECCA BENDHEIM

ART BY

SARAH ROSA GLICKMAN

Burlwood Books

Burlwood Books

Austin, Texas
BurlwoodBooks.com

First published in the United States of America
by Burlwood Books 2023

Text © 2023 Rebecca Bendheim
Interior & back cover art © 2023 Sarah Rosa Glickman

Cover design by Andrea Wofford
Front cover photo by Sean Petrie

ISBN 978-1-961853-01-0

1. Poetry 2. Relationships—Poetry 3. LGBTQ+—Poetry

For anyone who has felt alone on their journey—
we planned this party just for you.

CONTENTS

PART ONE: ROPES

PART TWO: GLITTER

PART THREE: FIRST TRIES

PART FOUR: DESIRE LINES

PART FIVE: SHE'S HOME

PART ONE: ROPES

It takes courage to grow up and become who you really are.

—E.E. Cummings

First Date

I am nine and she is thirteen,
and my mom is two booths over
at the local diner with the waiter
who loves to call my brother and me twins
but still,
this is it—
my first date with a girl.
She arrives three minutes late.
It feels like eighty.
She says she loves
all six of the drawings I made her
and laughs when I order the "Hungry Man's Breakfast."
I'd finish it a million times
if she'd never stop.

I am not that different now.
I still love a late-night diner
with a pretty girl.
I still get there on time,
present her with my poems.
Sometimes it still feels like
my mom is sitting around the corner.
I'd eat pancakes
till my throat closed up
to hear my girlfriend laugh
just one more time.

I think we are the most ourselves
when we are nine,
and I am always trying
to get back to her.

IMAGINARY FRIEND

On dark nights when you are alone
and your parents take your reading light,
you think about her.
You don't know what she looks like,
but you know she calls you her *best* friend,
and you call her yours.
You wear necklaces with little split hearts
so that everyone knows,
share tears, secrets, clothes,
stay up laughing at the stories
she tickles your ear with,
both in your twin bed
so no one will hear.
You tell her when your cereal is stale,
how many push-ups you did in gym class.
She runs into your house without knocking
and gets a popsicle from the freezer,
the kind your mom buys just for her.
Her tongue turns red
while you take an online quiz
that tells you what color your soul is.
You realize you don't even care
what color her soul is
or even if she wears necklaces
or likes popsicles
as long as she's yours.

You've wanted a girlfriend
since you were seven.

The most beautiful I've ever felt was in fifth grade, in a purple snowsuit, after a seventh-grade boy punched me four times in the chest. There were so many snow days then, our school name flashing across the bottom of the TV like a World Series win. You and I had our best friend tradition—meet halfway between our houses with tiny squirt bottles filled with food coloring and water to paint pictures in the snow.

When we got to the fence, we'd go quiet, try to sneak by before younger Max and older James climbed up to call us babies, Barbies, worse things, to say they'd fight us and how easily they'd win. You said they'd never really fight us. You didn't know I'd start it. But that day, Max's voice, "Babies, babies, babies," was a fork scraping Mom's nicest china, the squeak that makes half-digested rice and chicken roil in your stomach. I was armed only with color, but my stream of red spray stung Max's beady eyes, sent him screaming home to mommy, and James screaming over the fence to me.

It was quick and he wore gloves and the snow bed caught me on his first punch. I lay limp, chest open, let him swing again. Didn't scream and only cried when he was gone. You were gone, too. So I went home alone, shut my bathroom door, and didn't tell my mom. In the mirror, I was taller than I'd ever been before. My hair winter-dark and staticky, eyes still tear-stained, lips and cheeks flushed with cold. I peeled off my snowsuit and stood there in hand-me-down long underwear feeling really fucking beautiful.

So I didn't get it when my parents said, "Wear something nice," for church or temple or Thanksgiving dinner, and the choices were a pale dress or a long skirt, a shawl to cover my shoulders. They'd say, "You look nice." "You look beautiful." But I'd stand with the other girls by the church playground, tugging at our sleeves, watching the boys do the monkey bars over and over, wishing, sometimes, I was allowed to be mean.

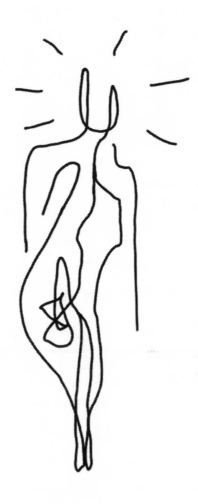

Ropes

The Home Depot rope section
was my sanctuary when I was eleven.
The burly men would smile when I asked for twelve feet,
but I'd stay serious, already picturing which trees I'd tie it to
in the web I was creating
so I could climb, traverse,
look out at the world.
My parents asked why I kept going,
using my birthday wishes up on ropes
instead of video games or clothes.
I didn't know then.
But eleven was my first foray
into the web of what to wear
and who to dance with,
"Your changing body"
and "Which boy do you like?"
It made sense that my birthday wish
was a web I made myself,
that maybe I just needed
something sturdy
to hold onto.

HOW IT STARTS

We're watching the winter assembly
from the back of the room today,
'cause in sixth grade, you can choose not to be in choir.
So we all chose not to be in choir.
But they're having fun up there,
dancing and singing and
waving to their parents.
Mine didn't come,
because why would they
when I'm not in choir?
So I'm watching and
wondering when
we stopped being little
when you scoot over to me
and put your hand over mine
on the gym floor.
I pull it away
and put my hand over yours.
You pull yours away
and put it right back
over mine—
a silent, little game
that's not so silent,
because Ms. Wakefield whisper-yells at us to "Be respectful,"
points to the empty spot next to where
she sits above us
in a fold-out chair.
So you scoot away again,
but when Ms. Wakefield's face is turned,
we still search for each other
and crack up every time
we catch each other's eye.

STALL CHANGER

"You're a stall changer," you said
after gym class the first week of seventh grade
sort of like a question,
sort of like an insult
(That's how everything you said sounded
back then).
"What are you scared of them seeing?"
"Nothing," I said,
and it wasn't a lie.
At home, I'd shower in my parents' bathroom,
the only one with a lock,
and dance in the mirror.
I loved the way my body was changing.

But in fifth grade, on a school field trip,
Victoria's bathing suit strap slipped.
Victoria, who raised her hand during the puberty talk
to say she'd gotten her period already
and we shouldn't be scared.
Who was on page 36 and 43 of the school yearbook.
Who I'd do anything to avoid sitting with.
Victoria, who I hated.
But really,
the more I liked her,
the more I hated myself.

Sitting on a girl's lap during play practice.
My camp counselor braiding my hair.
My teacher's hug the last day of fourth grade.
My friend's older sister who taught us dance in fifth—
I lost focus so much, I never left the back row.

It wasn't just Victoria.
It was me.

I was a stall changer.
But I wasn't scared of what they would see.
I was scared of what I would feel.

Ten years later, my friend Elizabeth crawls into my dorm bed
the morning they leave for California.
They are the kind of person who loves their friends hard,
even kisses them.
It's been years since I've let someone hug me
for more than two seconds.
But I am half asleep
and they are leaving,
so for the first time since Victoria,
I let myself
sink in.

You Knew First

In eighth grade,
you ask me who the most beautiful girl in the world is.
I think, *This is one of the good moments,*
till you say her name at school, in the locker room
before field hockey games,
just to see my cheeks burn, my stomach ache.
The worst thing about realizing I'm gay
is knowing you knew first.

You're Not Invited

I wish I noticed
the first day I got dressed
without your voice in my head.
"You're wearing that?"
"Innnnteresting."
"Are you gonna change?"
I wish I noticed,
so I could have thrown myself a party,
like the ones I never had,
because you convinced me
no one but you would come.

If You See Me at the Movies Alone

For a long time,
I only watched movies through her eyes.
Not because they were beautiful (which they were),
but because I was terrified
that I'd say the wrong thing
while we walked back to her car.

In *Mean Girls*,
they say not to buy a skirt without asking your friends first.
I didn't let my heart beat too fast,
didn't let a dream get too far from my gut,
didn't let a feeling pass from my chest
to my lips
without wondering first
if it would pass her test.

The longer I loved someone who didn't love me back,
the harder it was to find things worth loving.

So if you see me at the movies alone,
maybe you will understand
why I am making the most of $16.95,
eating even the last limp kernel of popcorn,
imagining every monologue
is spoken just to me,
letting no scene slip my mind,
because each character is mine, *all* mine,
and I love them
so hard—
like I love most things,
even though it's not cool to love most things.

But I don't think anyone should be ashamed
to love.

LOVE WE DIDN'T CALL LOVE

It was cloud 900.
I'd run home from your dorm,
the sky still pink, beginning,
your touch lingering.
I knew it would stay.
No parent approvals,
dates, flags, labels,
just walks by the lake under string lights
where you'd tell me about your sister
and I'd hold your hand.
Nights in the library
where you'd read my stories
and cry at the end.
We said I love you (the friend kind)
the first week we met,
and the April we were eighteen,
we were eating pretzels and
talking about the summer
when I told you I'd be happy forever
as long as you were here.
You leaned into me, shoulder to shoulder,
and we took Photo Booth pictures
on the giant school computer.
I still look at those sometimes
and miss how easy it was—
the love we didn't call love.
But you can never un-know.
My heart will never be as open
as before
the heartbreak
I couldn't call heartbreak.

FRIENDSHIP BREAKUP

After ignoring my texts for three weeks,
you give me a day together for my nineteenth birthday.

You reschedule it three times,
but at least you play "Wide Open Spaces" in the car,
and we scream it just like last year,
so loud that a motorcyclist swears at us
at a stoplight.

You don't touch me, not once.
When you pass me my smoothie,
you almost drop it on the mall floor,
so you won't have to brush my hand.
But at least you remember
I like the peanut butter one.

You went to this pumpkin patch last week
and posted a picture here with Holly.
You don't ask for a picture of us on the hay bales.
You take one just of me,
but at least you call me pretty.

We used to say we'd rather cuddle and talk
than do almost anything,
but today, you take me to the zoo,
the mall,
the pumpkin patch,
Jeni's Ice Cream,
on a hike by the lake
where we used to hold hands,
when a hundred days together
wasn't a gift,

but a given.

I say, "Thank you."
I don't say, *My heart is breaking.*
I don't ask
if this is goodbye.

Maybe

They want to talk about Ben
and Grant
and Ryan Gosling (again).
I'd rather talk about doorknobs
or toes
or bubblegum—
how people love to offer it,
stick it on desks and sidewalks,
smack it in your face.
The wrapping bright,
the bubbles huge and 90's movie cool,
but no matter the flavor,
to me, it has always been a little
bland
and sticky.
I spit it out before I come close
to making it POP on my tongue
and wonder,
Are they all lying?
Or maybe it's me
who is wrong.

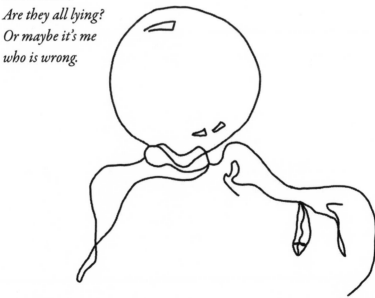

PART TWO: GLITTER

I'm like, so gay, dude.

—Kristen Stewart

QUESTIONING MY SEXUALITY AT THE CAMPUS VEGETARIAN CAFE

Am I gay?
I wonder as I stand in this line again
to get the veggie burger melt
but, really,
to hear you say my name.
That first day you rang me up,
I was too scared to say, "No pickles, please."
After melt thirty-seven,
they're my new favorite thing.
I didn't know
I could ever be a pickles girl.
But, I guess,
one sandwich
can change you.

OUT OF BODY EXPERIENCE

Having a secret
that pushes against my skin
but has to stay
        inside
     means there's no room in here
                 for me.

I watch myself from across the room.

Colors

Every appetizer I have with him
tastes like unseasoned, undipped artichoke.
So when he coronates me with the order,
I pick the first thing on the menu—
bacon-wrapped figs this time.
They come limp and beige
and taste like chewy nothing,
like his lips do
later in his gray car,
chapped with white skin-deaths
even after he smothers them
with a tube of unmarked clear gunk
he has in his glove box.

"That'll kill you," I say, turning away
while he blows silver smoke out his window
into nothingness.

My first morning in his non-dorm apartment,
I notice he has the kind of shades
that make everything impossibly
black.

But now,
across from her in a cafeteria booth,
shredded carrots are shots of orange zest through my veins.
I have to eat them one by one
and can't finish,
because my legs shake
with the urge to run—
bare feet tearing grass so green
it must be all preservatives,

like the strawberries I just ate,
the color of bubblegum toothpaste
spit in the sink,
like her lips
lit by the blue fire
she holds at the tip
of her cigarette.

Kiss me;
I'll die too.

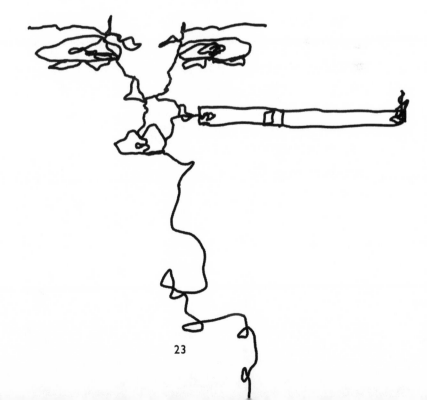

GLITTER

The boy who I kiss sometimes
is not my boyfriend
but wants to be.
He invites me to galas,
calls me gorgeous,
pulls out my chair.
Handsome in a corduroy blazer,
he presents his thesis on biology.
In the summers, he works at a ranch
out in Wyoming,
helps kids climb onto horses' backs.

The girl who I kiss sometimes
is not my girlfriend
and never will be.
She only likes girls "sexually."
She tries to punch the bouncer
for making us wait outside the bar
and asks me to be her character witness,
because she poured glitter into someone's eyes
when she was high on acid.
She lies to my face,
and I let her.

Some days, I still hope
that who I love
can be a choice.
But each late night
I spend waiting for her text,
it gets harder
to believe.

I am no longer the girl
who doesn't let such a silly thing
as love
get in the way of
"more important matters."
I am no better than the rest of them.
Skipping stats class
to watch her smoke behind the library.
Skipping the birthday dinner,
because she said maybe
she'd stop by.
Miserable.
Desperate.
Giddy.
Blinded
by glitter.

If...

If Glinda and Elphaba were gay,
For Good would be the greatest breakup song
of our time.

If Kat Stratford were gay,
the spiky haired girl from the rock band
would eye her in the audience.
Kat would write *her* a poem instead,
on a bar napkin,
and throw it onto the stage during the last song.
They'd make out in the dressing room
and fall in love over readings of *The Bell Jar*
at the lesbian bookstore.

If Viola Hastings and Olivia were gay,
Olivia would run onto the field
and, just before the flash,
make out with Viola in front of everyone,
showing the crowd that kissing girls,
like playing soccer,
isn't just for boys.
They'd hook up in the country club bathroom
during the debutante ball
and then become gym girlfriends,
falling in love over deep talks
while spotting each other
at the weight station.

If Jo March were gay,
Professor Behr would be just a writing partner
who'd help her get a scholarship to Mount Holyoke,
where she'd argue with a girl in her class,

but then realize she couldn't stop thinking about her.
They'd take the train to Concord,
and she'd fall asleep on Jo's shoulder.
Jo would try her hardest to stay still
while she looked out at the blurry fall leaves
and wondered how to tell Laurie and her sisters.

If Lindsey Lohan had been allowed to date a hot girl DJ
without it being called a mental breakdown.
If *I Kissed a Girl* had ended in
definitely being "in love tonight."
If Emily in *Pretty Little Liars* had a girlfriend
who did not die or lie or try to drown her.
If...
If...
If...

Would it have been any easier?

How I Came Out in One Breath to My Friend in the Car at 8AM

Hey you know how that guy asked me to formal but I said no my sisters will be in town well that was a lie I just really didn't want to go kissing him is like eating dried-out chicken sorry that was weird speaking of weird sometimes I feel like there are daggers in my stomach around this girl from my psych class I want to be closer to her but not in a friend way in a crawl-into-her-skin way so I think I don't like boys only girls no I don't need a tissue I'm not crying can you drop me off right here? No it's okay I can walk to class I want to walk just drop me off
please

THE JEWEL

I present you with the jewel
I have been polishing.
"See how it sparkles
in the sun?"
You ask,
"How will you get around
this boulder?"

You won't face it,
not directly.
If you did, you would see
its colors,
how it fits in the palm of my hand.

Please don't be scared.
I am going to have a beautiful life.
I already do.

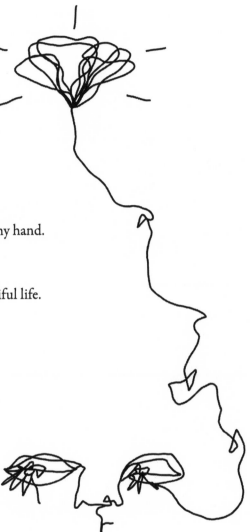

What My Queer Therapist Sent to My Professors the Week I Came Out

Our office received documentation that Rebecca has experienced a
(crush)
(reckoning)
(major life upgrade)
personal crisis.

She may miss
(who she was before)
(Morgan, who made it weird)
(feeling like she fit anywhere)
classes.

*Her academics may be impacted, and as a result, Rebecca may
require*
(7,000 years of alone time)
(Everyone to just shut up)
(The pretty girl from the cafe to just kiss her already and make all
this worth it)
some accommodations regarding coursework.

You will hurt all over.
You will wonder if you're making it up.
It will take months for you to say it
without your skin crawling,
and years for you to really fall in love.

But a crisis
isn't just an emergency.
It comes from the Greek word for "decision"
and came to mean the turning point of a disease,
the moment of clarity

when the doctors knew the patient's fate.

Telling people who you are
is not vanity.
You are choosing
to live.

COMING OUT PARTY

The weeks before I came out,
I'd say goodnight to my friends at the college bar
and walk thirty minutes to the gay club alone.
I'd sit at the bar and watch the people dance,
then go to the bathroom and hope someone would ask me
to pass paper towels under the door
or tell them if their eyeliner was even.
On the dark walk home,
I'd think about how every day of my life
someone had known where I was,
until now,
and I'd feel like a tiny speck
floating
in a never-ending universe—
both so alone
and so full of maybes.

Tonight would be different.
I had told ten friends.
One was praying for me,
but nine were coming
to my favorite restaurant with the mini brie grilled cheeses
and flutes of tomato cream soup,
curtains that closed your booth,
and a place to dock your phone so it played through the speakers.

One friend bought champagne for the whole table.
One wrote me a letter.
One made a playlist of "coming out" music.
So I didn't get why
I didn't feel like celebrating.
Maybe it was the music—a mix of Lady Gaga and Ariana Grande

when I'd been listening to Hayley Kiyoko.
Maybe it was the questions—
how *things* worked with a girl.
All I'd tried was one kiss.
Or maybe it was that my crush,
a bi girl from class,
arrived twenty minutes late in paint-covered jeans,
gave me a face-sized sunflower,
looked around at my friends,
and said she had to get going.

I think it was realizing
that every day of my life
someone had known, had understood
who I was,
but not now.
I was alone inside myself.
Maybe I always had been.

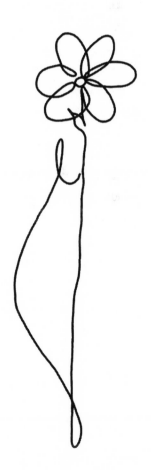

I carried the sunflower like a child
that whole night at the college bar
and then put it in my Brita pitcher
so it would have the cleanest water.
I needed it to survive.
It felt like my only proof
that any of this was real.

Things You Do in Frat House Bathrooms

Mummify your tampon and hide it in your purse,
because they didn't think to have a trash can.

Unscrew your Adderall bottle
but don't swallow the pill at first,
in case you change your mind.
You promised yourself you'd only take them while studying,
but too late,
it's dissolving, bitter on your tongue.

Throw up from tequila.
From food poisoning after that burger
made by a nineteen-year-old
who grew up with a chef.
Or from shame.
Wash your face after.
Let soap sting your eyes.

Kiss me,
even though you are "straight,"
even though people are knocking.

IF A LESBIAN SITS IN A CAFE AND NO ONE IS AROUND TO SEE HER...

If I wear these boots,
rainbow pin,
roll my T-shirt sleeves.
If I bleach my hair,
pierce my nose,
wear shorts down to my knees.
If I wait
in this cafe,
equality sticker
and oat milk latte,

will you see me?

Am I real
if you don't see me?

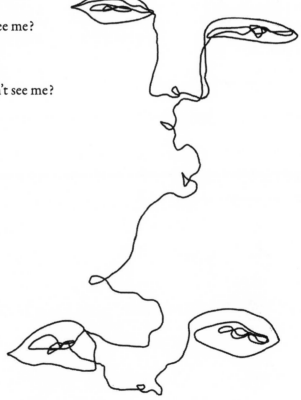

TOO LATE

Three years of therapy,
thirteen journals,
one thousand "All Too Well" streams,
one million steps
alone around the lake
to go from *Why am I not good enough?*
to *You were just not ready.*
For my stomach to stay put
when I saw you at parties.
But now you are here and drunk,
light touch on my shoulder—
"Can I tell you a secret?"
just like at eighteen,
and I say, "Yes."
It's your dreams.
These days, they are all pretty girls—
kissing!
"Too late," I say and run,
because I can't be thrown back
to the start.
But I want you to know
that I meant it was too late for us.
Not for you.
The world is a little bit kinder now,
and I hope the first pretty girl you love
is a little kinder than you were, too.

I Remember Every Lesbian Couple I Ever Saw

The first is at Barnes and Noble where I work and am supposed to be shelving, but really, I am delving into the only lesbian book we have. It's Nashville where the Christian section is three times the Fiction section, and the gay books are in the back by the bathroom. This book is trashy and problematic, but every day I pray they still have it, that no one buys it before I have the courage to.

But one day, I'm leaving out the back entrance on my ten-minute break, when I see them—two girls, one pulling the other up the down escalator, their hair dyed the same color in a way that makes me think of them dunking each other's heads in the sink. They share the same step, stand so close, but then see me staring and let go. I think maybe I am in an alternate universe, my body bubbling like too much champagne, heart racing like *that could be me one day*. When I finally get to leave, I buy that lesbian book and take it home with me.

I don't see another lesbian couple for over a year. Not until after I come out, and my sorority sisters say I am the first gay person they've ever met and ask me questions like, "How do lesbians have sex?" I tell them things I learned on the internet. I don't see them until after my mom tells me about her friend Jane's son who's "straight now" and maybe I should wait to come out just in case. And I don't see them when I move to the Bay and the only gay people I see are tech guys at San Francisco Pride.

But then, I'm at the Berkeley Bowl, lost trying to find the cereal, when I see them—a girl with short hair smiling while piling fruit up on the belt. Another girl runs out with a box of almond milk, shouts, "Wait! You paid at Trader Joes!" The first girl laughs, says, "No, I swear it was you," and they kiss and everything freezes... I am alone in a grocery store trying to hide my tears, because I never find the cereal aisle, but I do find out that, in 21 years, I have never seen two women kiss.

After that, it's like they're everywhere. Maybe my eyes weren't trained before, but there are the middle-aged women who kiss during the credits of *Call Me by Your Name*. There are the old women laying in the grass by Jack London Square, flowers in their curly hair. Teenagers on a first date at Lake Merritt, blushing and scared. Two girls with shaved heads and cutoff shirts trying to share a skateboard in San Francisco and me, trying not to stare. And then there are my own friends who dance and kiss like the world might end and can't see I'm starstruck every time.

Because somehow, now, I'm surrounded by people who wear their love on their sleeve and hold hands, even when it's scary, and kiss like it's breathing. I hope they know I see them. I hope they know I am not staring because they are gross or weird, but because I know it's the most fearless and beautiful thing.

So thank you to the purple-haired girls in the back of Barnes and Noble, the women at the Berkeley Bowl, the nose-ringed girls dancing close in that record store, who kiss without ever looking over their shoulders.

I see you. Someday, I'll be one of you.

And soon, when I go back to a place where people like us are erased, I will know how to be brave. And I will be.

Maybe II

You say you'll pick me up at the airport
but never show,
so I wait three hours,
take the 5AM train to your door.
You don't have a mattress yet,
so we have sex on your floor,
and then you say, "I can't do this.
I only date jaded girls
who I can't hurt.
You see me as better than I am."
I stand, take my bag,
and look at you down there
on your makeshift bed,
but see all of us—
queer girls with no soft place to land—
called sinners, liars,
entertainment,
waiting for cars
that will never come.
Maybe we are too damaged to ask more of each other,
to ever make
such a grandiose ask
as love.

PART THREE: FIRST TRIES

You kept me like a secret, but I kept you like an oath.

—Taylor Swift

HAIR TIE

I wish you'd left earrings,
a watch,
a retainer, even.
I can't text you,
I found your hair tie.
Come back to get it.
I need to see you
just one more time.

Australia on My Birthday

Maybe you are on vacation
somewhere like Australia,
somewhere it is still yesterday.
It's tomorrow in Australia, I think
but won't check,
because it is 11pm,
and I want to believe
you might still text me.
I wish I knew
love has no **room**
for excuses.

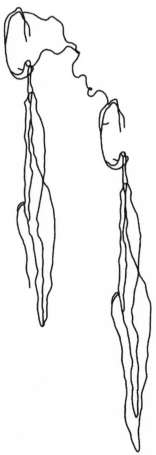

Hate Letter
after *10 Things I Hate About You*

I hate the way you blame dumb things you say on your horoscope.
I hate that you buy kombucha and then get mad that you're broke.
I hate how you say that I can't play pop music in the car,
and then you quote Ed Sheeran once you've taken off my bra.

I hate those hanging dice on the mirror of your Camry.
I hate that you sent me articles on why not to eat candy.
Honestly, you've got no right to tell me to regret
my froyo when we both know that's not your last cigarette.

And, on that note, I really, really hate your blue light vape,
and I think smoking Hookah is sooooo 2008.
I hate how you're so damn proud of your Samsung phone.
Wow! It charges *and* plays music
and will probably explode.

I seriously hate that you cried when we broke up,
so that somehow I felt bad for you when I was getting dumped.
But most of all I hate that though it's been half a year,
I can't hate you,
 and I guess I should probably be more clear...

I hate those dice 'cause they remind me
of that time you lost your keys.
While we waited hours for AAA,
you told me you liked me.
Smelling smoke makes me think back to how you'd try to make me cough,
and how I never would admit that I thought it was really hot.
You bought that vape back in July, so I could breathe while in your car,
and I remember driving, aimless, watching fireworks from afar.

I can't even drink kombucha 'cause it makes me think of you,
of the first time that I tried it and spit it out outside Whole Foods.

I still turn off the radio when Ed Sheeran comes on,
'cause when I played guitar, you used to ask to hear his songs.
And even though I've always thought that horoscopes were dumb,
I believed you when you told me that yours said we'd fall in love.
So I guess I wish you'd call me
on that stupid Samsung phone,
'cause I hate that I'm not over you
and I'd love if you came home.

RECIPE FOR AN EMOTIONAL SUPPORT LESBIAN

This recipe is only three ingredients.
So easy, I've seen it made a million times.
Guaranteed to improve
any straight girl's life.

You will need
one straight girl
whose hand lingers by your neck
after a hug.

One unavailable boyfriend (or almost boyfriend)
who asks if she is on her period
if she expresses
any slightly inconvenient emotion.

And one lesbian
who has been rejected and shamed
so many times,
she'd rather lift moving boxes,
have long talks
and longer hugs
with a girl
who could never date her in the first place.

Now the straight girl
is your active ingredient.
At 2AM, she will beg the lesbian to come over
after a fight with her boyfriend
and tell her she's the only person in the world
who understands.

When the boyfriend cancels on their park date,

the straight girl will ask the lesbian instead.
She will take her on a shopping trip
and come out of dressing rooms half-naked
to ask if she looks good.
The lesbian can't stare too long
but must always say yes
and carry the bags.
When the straight girl moves into the boyfriend's apartment,
she will call again.
The lesbian will come over with a toolbox
and tissues,
because she knows any kind of leaving
makes the straight girl sad.
On nights out,
the straight girl will buy the lesbian drinks
and call her hot
and maybe even kiss her in the bathroom
when she's drunk enough.
The lesbian will start to hope
and will try to crush it,
but when the couple is on vacation in Europe,
she will walk their dogs and house sit
and look at their photo on the mantel.
For the first time, she will let herself wonder,
Why can't it be me?
When they come home engaged,
she will speak now
instead of holding her peace.
It will take everything in her
to say how she feels.
The straight girl will act surprised
and say, "Aw, that's sweet,

but I only see you
as a friend."

NOTE: This recipe has been recalled.
If you have ever been an emotional support lesbian,
you are entitled to emotional compensation.

LOVE DOESN'T

have to be requited
to be beautiful.

IT'S FINALLY HAPPENING IT'S FINALLY HAPPENING
IT'S FINALLY HAPPENING IT'S FINALLY HAPPENING
IT'S FINALLY HAPPENING IT'S FINALLY HAPPENING
IT'S FINALLY HAPPENING IT'S FINALLY HAPPENING
IT'S FINALLY HAPPENING IT'S FINALLY HAPPENING
IT'S FINALLY HAPPENING IT'S FINALLY HAPPENING
IT'S FINALLY HAPPENING IT'S FINALLY HAPPENING
this isn't how i hoped it would feel

WHAT PEOPLE WANTED TO KNOW ABOUT MY HIGH SCHOOL BOYFRIEND

Is there a boy in your life?
What's he look like?
Does he play sports?
Does he have siblings?
What does he want to be
when he grows up?
Is he close with his family?
Can we meet them?
Which of these five restaurants
do you think they'd like most?
Does he have allergies?
Where does he want to go to college
in three years?
Do you love him?
Is he kind?
Are you mad? Why?
I'm just curious.

She is kind,
and I might love her.
I wish you'd ask.

WHEN YOU WAIT (IT TASTES BETTER)

My girlfriend and I are making out in the CVS parking lot
when she stops me
and tells me it's almost ten,
that my mom will want us back
with the aloe vera and medicine
she sent us out for over an hour ago.

"Nooo," I say and set off the windshield wipers of our rental car,
wrapping my leg around her waist, trapping her,
and thinking how she feels like...an apricot—
soft and sweet and my favorite color.
How she tastes like the first time I tried champagne,
before I'd ever had a hangover,
and wondered if it would lift me like Charlie—
high off running through a magical place
he'd only ever seen on TV,
his heart too wild to resist
a fizzy lift
into the sky.

I lay in her lap as she drives us back,
talks nonsense about how a manual is almost too easy,
and there's nothing good on the radio,
and do my parents like her?
I'm not really listening.
Just thinking how I haven't told her yet
that my mom won't let us share a bed.
She's already moved a twin sized cot
into the room I share with my sister.

But when my girlfriend sees it,
she tells my mom she likes the tiny flowers sewn into the comforter,

brushes her teeth with my little sister,
and in the middle of the night,
I still my pounding heart
and sneak into her bed.
She turns in her sleep
and tucks her hand under my Taylor Swift T-shirt
from 2007.

And I'm thinking how fifteen is the gay twenty-three,
or sixty, or ninety-two, or however long it takes for you
to get to a place
where your girlfriend tastes like an apricot
and not some sort of revolution
or revelation
or statement.

I'm thinking how I spent so long
wishing I could fall in love in Algebra II,
not on an app or in a dark room.
That my "first time" was after prom, not in the closet of a dive bar
with an Ariana Grande song and an angry bartender as background music.

But now I'm twenty-three, bringing my girlfriend, who's almost thirty,
home with me,

and my mom is treating us like we're seventeen,
not because she's scared of us,
but because she's never gotten to do this with me,
since I spent so long thinking love was something made up to sell movies,
so many hours googling if at thirteen, at nineteen, at twenty-three
it was too late for me.

But now, I wake up as the sun rises to sneak back to my childhood bed,
and when I kiss her good morning, I think:
It tastes better when you wait.

There's no law saying I can't still be impressed that my girlfriend's good at driving,
no reason I needed to understand the love songs on Taylor Swift's first album
the first three hundred times.
And if you go back and watch *Willy Wonka* grown up, with new eyes,
you'll see that Grandpa Joe
had the best time
of all.

CURSED

"You are going to break my heart"
is a curse
I don't want any part in.
What if, for once,
I don't want to be the clumsy one?
What if I want to step slowly,
take wide turns,
no shortcuts,
hold it tight (but not too tight),
give it just the right amount of rain and sun?
For once, I'd like to not give up,
to wait out the storms in a woodland cabin,
keeping it warm (but not too close)
by the fire.
I can't promise I won't trip,
let it slip through **my hands.**
But I promise I will **love** it as hard (and as soft)
as I can.

I Wear...

Your high school T-shirts,
too-big sneakers,
too-small shorts.
Your hair tie
that breaks after two tugs around,
dirty socks,
underwear,
old sweatshirts.
I can never be close enough.
I'd wear your skin if you'd let me.

DRIVING AFTER THE CRASH

I don't remember the crash.
I remember the smoke, the siren sounds, the aftermath, my car speakers
still blasting the same song as if to say *That was less than three minutes of
your life.*

The next day at work, my boss says, "You're so lucky you didn't get hurt,"
and tells me I'm late,
because he doesn't know there were a thousand more crashes in my mind
on the way there.

I don't remember sixteen,
but I can't forget him closing that door.
Never said, "No," but I did say, "Go slow,"
and when I came home upset,
my friends said
it's normal to cry, normal to hurt, normal not to like it.
I was too sixteen, too relieved to see that it shouldn't be.

He said, "You are my girlfriend, I can do whatever I want with you."
You say, "You are my girlfriend, we can wait however long you want."

And you wait with me
through every "I'm not ready,"
take off my clothes like they're breakable,
hold my shaky hands until they're still,
on a side street,
'cause I couldn't drive in the rain.

You—a forgiving blue sky,
an empty Sunday highway,

Route 1 in a world full of 5s.
You don't mind that I pull over and let every single car go by,
and when I wait to turn left through three red lights,
you turn up the radio
so I won't hear the honking
and whisper in my ear,
"I am just happy to be here."

My family dog is terrified of boxes,
so ever since we adopted her,
our holidays and birthdays have been all in bags.
It feels bigger than patience
when you hold my hesitation like it's a gift
and sit by me as I drive after the crash.

Everyone deserves to be loved like that.

TV

There is a scene in the movie *Babe*
where the grandfather builds a dollhouse with his weathered hands.
The whole family gathers to watch the little girl's joy
as she tears the wrapping paper.
She shrieks,
but not the good kind,
screams, "It's the wrong one!
I wanted the one I saw on TV!"
The old man's hurt only shows
in his stare, unblinking.
She doesn't even turn
to see it.

I come home to candles laid across the room,
lotion on your hands, ready to ease my long-day strain.
The kind of love I saw on TV,
but I just want to sleep
anywhere but here,
suffocated
by fake-floral smoke.
The only kindness I have in me
is to let them continue to burn.

When I re-watch that dollhouse scene,
I will the little girl to *smile*,
say *thank you*
like I couldn't.
I tell her to pick up the dollhouse,
feel how heavy.
I warn her that the one of her dreams
may feel empty
in her arms.

ALL YOU NEED TO GO

You don't need a flying hairdryer
or screaming in the kitchen,
"different values"
or heart-eyes texts
with the new intern.
All you need to go
is the tiniest
    no
deep in your chest.

Tell her.
It will not go away.
She can feel it already.

New Crush

A week after my breakup,
my sister asks if I have any new crushes.
I say, "I'm not sure I'm ready."
She waits.
I say, "There's this girl.
I don't really know her though.
I just saw her at the bar.
A friend of a friend."
"What do you like about her?" my sister asks.
"I guess that she was dancing,
and it wasn't a dancing kind of bar.
That she smiled at me like we were friends
when we weren't.
That she was wearing sneakers, the running kind,
that looked really comfortable."
"So, she's just like you?" my sister asks.
I protest first.
Then I realize—
I hope she is right.

Love and *Love*

After years of "love you"
(the friend kind),
"I *love* you" rolls in like monsoon rain
pelting me in the center of your field,
no escape from knowing
how close our arms are,
from counting the ways you laugh,
wondering what you would do
if I moved that lock of hair,
tucked it back.
Suddenly, I can't bear to miss
even one fraction
of your face.

You know
because you know me,
and we dance in the majesty of it—
love and *love*, cracking the sky open.
Us on that seesaw years ago.
Us now, fused to each other,
dancing in the everywhere-ness of it—
us and *us*
soaked in forevers,
those behind
and those ahead.

But I know
because I know you.
You are shivering now,
and I am parched.
How could love and *love*
not add up

to something?
It did.
It *did.*
Just not quite
enough.
I can't remember
the last time you laughed.
I am only making you colder.

Losing *love*
means losing love.
There's no escape
from the nowhere-ness of it,
the listlessness
of the one-sided seesaw ride.
The screaming silence
when the rain
stops.

No History of Tenderness

is worth today's bloodshed.

I FINISHED OUR SHOW (I'M SORRY)

I finished our show in two days,
because I watched every time I would usually talk to you.
I can't believe it was him.
Do you think she died?
Do you think there'll be a season 2?
It was my first time in almost a year
watching TV without you there,
laughing at the smallest things,
crying at the smallest things,
while I sat there like the zombie I am
and probably wished that I were reading.
But this episode, I cried like nine times,
laughed like a crazy person,
and talked to myself,
screamed to myself
at the jump-scares.
It kills me to say
I liked it better that way.
Do you remember that day you cleaned my room while I was at work,
folded my pants into little rolls,
so I could see them all in my drawer?
Well, you were right.
It was easier.
But, for some reason, I can't keep it like that.
I can't fit them all, and I have no idea how you did it.
So my life will just have to be
a little harder
from now on.
I'm wearing the shirt I gave you once,
after the first time we said, "I love you."
The last time, I traded you

for a shirt I liked less.
The worst part is
I think you knew what I was doing.
I think you knew I'd be laying here
in my own bed,
in my favorite T-shirt,
glad to have space next to me
for my Kindle and water bottle,
hoping your show is better
without me too.
Hoping your life is easier.

MAYBE III

She writes me notes
and hides them in my suitcase,
makes me curry,
and tells me I'm going to be
better than okay,
even when I am leaving her.
Yet I am leaving her.
If this is who I can't love enough,
then maybe love is something
I shouldn't even try.

PART FOUR: DESIRE LINES

Often we see queerness as a deprivation, but when I looked at my life, I saw that queerness demanded an alternative innovation from me; I had to make alternative routes.

—Ocean Vuong

Fall Air

When I walk down that aisle at the airport,
the one where people wait to pick up their loved ones,
I keep my head up,
pretend one of those babies
with their wiggling arms,
those old women with laugh lines and roses,
preteens with magic marker signs
is waiting for me.
Pretend so hard
the drivers with white boards eye me
and say, "Natasha?" "Cortez?"
So hard I'm surprised when I get to the end
and no one's claimed me.
It's not till I'm in my driveway,
where I sit for almost an hour
half listening to guilty pleasure songs,
because no one is waiting for me inside,
that I remember breaking up with my girlfriend
because she wanted to get married,
my mom crying
when I moved to California,
that I live hundreds of miles
from anyone who's known me longer than a year.
But when I walk down my street each day,
I see so many people like me
walking dogs,
wandering,
coming off the summer of our childhoods
like monarchs—migrating,
preparing for our winters and springs—
and, for now,
alone in my car,

playing that song no one else likes,
windows down at midnight
outside my empty apartment,
I imagine there are millions of us
with no one to pick us up from the airport,
thinking the fall air
feels so damn good.

Brownies and Pizza and Jesus

Of course we believe you.
You get us when we're young.
"Join our club.
There are brownies and pizza,
and you never have to die."

"Listen," you say.
"The music you are lost in—
that's Him
saying He'll love you forever."
You don't add the footnotes
till later.

You will never die
if
 you give up
much of what
gives you will to live.

He will always love you
if
you give up
the love down here,
the kind you can touch.

I asked a minister once—
"Why ignore so many rules
and follow this one?"

He said those rules were Old Testament,
old news.
"What about women speaking in church," I asked,

"like I am doing right now?
What about divorce?"

He said, "I don't know."

I tried to imagine it,
not knowing
the restless midnight shame,
the kids turned away from home
and school
and homeless shelters,
the teens who choose to die
rather than meet the fate
you set out for them,
the fate you base off
I
don't
know.

I find god in the trees now,
the way they stretch
toward the ground and sky in equal measure.
In the music
at the Girls Rock concert,
green-haired eight-year-olds
slamming on electric guitars
to their screaming parents.
And yes, in brownies and pizza,
how they are only so delicious
because there will be
a final bite.

THE RIGHT QUESTION

My physical therapist says it's rare
to be both a foot slapper
and a heel striker,
to wear the soles of my shoes right off.
He asks, "Why are you so hard on the ground?"
My regular therapist asks:
"Why are you so hard on yourself?"

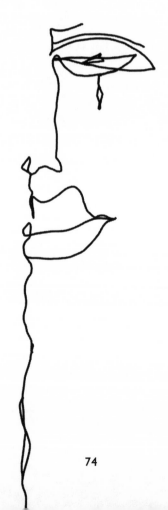

THE RIGHT QUESTION II

When I wondered, *Do they like me?*
I lost myself.
When I wondered, *Do I like them?*
I lost them.
When I wondered, *Do I like myself*
when I'm with them?
I found both.

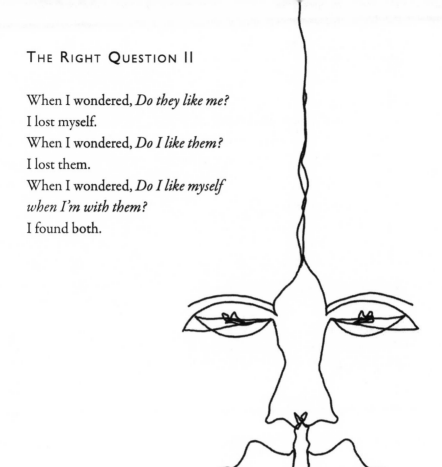

Desire Lines

"There are three ways to design walkways,"
my overexcited tour guide explained,
looking over the wide library lawn
of the seventh college I visited the year I was sixteen.
It was full of winding, white cement paths
as random as those canvasses
elephants paint with their trunks.

"First, you can make them straight and precise,
perfectly centered and aligned.
But there will always be people
who take shortcuts.
Architectural rebels, you might say."
He chuckled.
"Your perfect grass
will soon be riddled with ugly dirt paths
called 'desire lines.'"

"Second, you can try to predict
how the people will move.
You can use math. Physics. But the thing is—
you can never truly know.
You can spend millions on equations, analysis
and still end up with dirt."

"But here," he motioned to the lawn.
"We took the third option.
We built these buildings
and then we waited
for *years*
for the dirt to appear.
To see where the students' feet took them
when they were free of rules and guidance.

Once the desire lines were deep
and sure,
we paved."

I thought, *That's what I want.*
But even that college
was filled with precise paths
it hurt to follow.
I was terrified
I'd ruin the grass.

It wasn't until years later
that I found myself surrounded by people
who follow their desire lines.
Architectural rebels
of love
who realize our own paths are more fun
and become
architectural rebels
of space
and time,
career
and family,
art
and style,
and life.
And, because of them,
I am no longer afraid
of a little dirt.

What Chloe Taught Me

Love with

You amaze me.
Take my umbrella.
Come here.
Let me help.

but not

That hurt.
Don't say that, please.
Can we talk?
Can we leave?

can never go beneath
the surface.

LAST TIME, AT THE GAY BAR
after the Colorado Springs shooting

Look both ways.
Watch the entrance.
Your first time at a gay bar,
you want everyone to see you,
just not anyone you know.
Drag queens flip
to electric bass synth,
but your unscuffed docs
forgot how to dance
till smoke billows from the ceiling,
an old school magic show.
You're free now,
dancing on your own.

Your 86th time at a gay bar,
drag queens flip.
Your girlfriend spins you
across sticky floors.
But this time,
when smoke billows from the ceiling,
you wonder, with the bass thundering,
would you hear a bang?
In the convoluted air,
would you know which way
to run?
Look both ways.
Watch the entrance.
Where's the entrance?

Sisters

We sing *Our Song* underwater,
pop up at the pool wall and see
if we are at the same part.
We aren't,
but we try again, closer each time
until we are heavy-breathed and tired,
sprawled out on the grass.

We yell out movie initials
and try to read each other's minds,
play Twenty Questions on hikes.
Each time, I choose a person we've met just once,
like the waiter from the road trip
when you dropped me off at college
who dropped tartar sauce on my lap.
I tried to bottle up your laugh,
so it would last until Thanksgiving.

We pick cards out of a red box,
guess what you fear most,
what I'd do with a million dollars,
what song describes this chapter of your life.
When we were little, we played "Lifeguard."
I can't count the times
you've brought me back
to the surface.

All our games
ask the same things:
Do you know me?
Do you still love me?
Do you understand?

Yes.
Yes.
Yes.
Always.
Yes.

THE EIGHT-TOED CAT
for Noah

When we were twenty-three,
before real jobs or girlfriends
or friends besides each other,
we'd walk two miles each evening
to get to-go margaritas
and visit the eight-toed cat.
He'd slink out of the alley like he was waiting for us
but never came close enough to touch.
He'd sit tall, his front leg outstretched
to show off that paw,
those eight strange
and gorgeous toes.
He watched over us
when you told me the dream you had
when you were nine—
you, a man, next to your pregnant wife.
When I wrote that breakup speech in my phone notes
and practiced the poem
for my first show.
When you gave yourself
that gorgeous name,
spinning the butterfly pin on your jean jacket.

Our lives got full,
and we moved to parts of the city
with cleaner alleys
and never said goodbye,
but I bet he's still there
showing the new queers
on their long walks to nowhere
that there is power in the things
we can't quite yet understand.

ETIQUETTE
    for *The Club*

At 3AM, the last night of Christian camp,
we shake each other awake,
run down to the field,
use our finely-honed flag etiquette skills
to raise our rainbow contraband
into the sky.
This is the best part, I think
when we perform a made-up ritual,
hold hands and spin around the pole,
fall dizzy and cackling into the dirt,
but it's not.

It's four hours later,
when, from my favorite sunrise-watching spot,
I see a nine-year-old notice it
then race down the path.
She thinks she is alone,
does a happy dance,
then, head tall and hand on her heart,
says the pledge of allegiance.

FOR ME

I love the way your toes clench,
anticipation in your chest.
You have so many places to go.
I love how easily you smile,
the scratch in your voice from speaking louder
with each syllable
that makes your heart hum.
There are so many things
you still haven't done.
I love that you run places when you are alone
and try hobbies so new
you can't pronounce their names.
I love how it only takes you a day
to call a new place home,
but how you still call your best friend from second grade
every year on her birthday.
I love how you sing and dance on your bike,
like you are both a superstar
and a roaring stadium,
only stopped by red lights.
You don't need to be anything more
than this.

Maybe IV

Why I Can't Find Love (from my journal the summer after I came out)

Maybe
- I'm "looking for it"
- I'm too dependent
- I'm too independent
- My standards are too high
- I don't look gay enough
- I have awful gaydar
- I don't pay attention
- I'm scared
- I wear earphones too much

You're right about one thing—
you aren't paying attention.

Look:
There you are holding Elizabeth's hand
while they get a teaspoon tattoo.

Your first pride,
you bat your rainbow false eyelashes
while you lie to the NYU dorm police
and sneak six new friends
and twenty-four White Claws
into your room.

That's you in Brooklyn
getting cheap margaritas,
just making the 4 train
where you share earphones,

listen to the cast recording of *Fun Home,*
then walk down every aisle of The Strand
and dare each other to talk to that shaggy-haired girl.
She leaves before either of you get her number,
but that's not the point.

You have never had a summer like this,
free and full
of people who see you.
More will come.
Right now,
let this be enough.

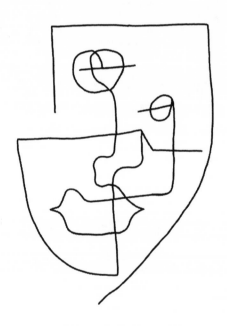

PART FIVE: SHE'S HOME

When you spend so much time just intensely wanting something, and then you actually get the thing? It's magic... It's butterflies and haziness and heart eyes, but underneath all that, there's this bass line of I can't believe this. I can't believe this is me. *I can't quite articulate the sweetness of that feeling. It's finding out the door you were banging on is finally unlocked. Maybe it was unlocked the whole time.*

– Becky Albertalli

How We Met

It didn't happen
>   once I'd given up,
>   after I loved myself,
>   when I least expected it.

It happened
>   on a regular night
>   at my regular bar
>   in my roommate's borrowed clothes.

You were dancing on your own
in cutoff overalls.
I chickened out the first time.
An hour later,
pulled my hair up tight.
"I like your overalls."
(Not even a good pickup line)
"Want to dance?"
(Not even creative)
You were tipsy.
I was shaky.
We couldn't keep the beat.

There was no magic in
>   that place
>   that night,
>   even you
>   or me.

It came on our separate walks home.
When your friends asked
and so did mine.
When we both looked out
at the lit-up city
unable to conceal our smiles.

MORNING TEST

My friends used to ask,
"Did he pass the morning test?"
They meant did I wake up,
hear his sleep sounds,
smell his morning breath,
and want to *stay*?
No.
Never.
The sun and I wake together
and don't waste time
setting fire to the day.
An impossible test,
I thought till I saw her
just past midnight,
setting fire to the dance floor.
It was already morning,
and I already wanted
so many more.

First Date

After we kissed next to the dumpster,
you said, "Now I want to walk you back to your car,"
and we laughed,
because I had just walked you back to yours.
I didn't know how to say,
I would have stayed all night with you,
walking in circles.

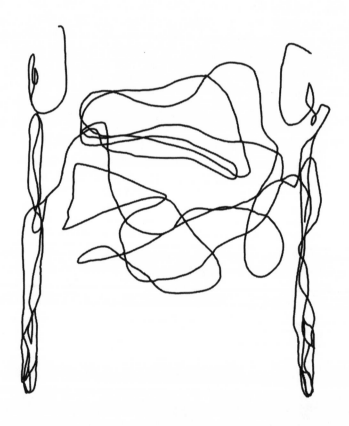

Second Date

"Didn't you say you were an anxious driver?"
Yes,
but tonight, a siren was a sweet song.
The ambulance a flurry of fairy lights.
I pulled to the side, right hand on your thigh,
and we watched it rumble past, then went on our way.
Dark turns like woodland paths.
I missed one when you sang along to "Dylan Thomas,"
took the long way around,
then stopped in front of your building, clicked my flashers on,
and kissed you on the disco curb.
A girl who makes me want to trust the world
just a little bit more.

THIRD DATE

We sang "Cowboy Take Me Away" on the ride to the Thai food
truck,
and when we got home, I made you try on my uncle's cowboy hat.
It looked so good that I led you by your shoulders to my bathroom
mirror
where I saw us together for the first time.
This morning, I stalked your Spotify
 and saw you added "Cowboy Take Me Away" to your playlist for
the plane.
So maybe I'll let myself wish
that next time you'll take me with you.

FIREWORKS

"I don't know if I feel fireworks with Cam,"
Belly says in *The Summer I Turned Pretty*.
That night, we stared at the sunset too long
and got stuck biking home in the dark.
I couldn't see where I was going,
but I knew that you would follow.

      HF!JJDSJDD!%%FF"#GF^&((

The boom rattled our bodies.
Shards of green light
struck the path, so close.
"Let's go!"
We took cover, dragging our bikes through grass.
I touched your arm,
and we were shaken but okay,
maybe a little electric.
I still haven't stopped
feeling a little electric.
When you feel fireworks,

           you'll know.

Silver Linings Girl

The card machine wasn't working at Biderman's Deli,
so we got our sandwiches for free
and said they tasted even better
when we heated up the leftovers for dinner.
Then we biked the trail
and crossed under the South Congress bridge
just as the bats flew out
to start a new night.
People drive, fly from all over to see this,
and we were here by accident—
you, dusk-golden in my tie-dye T-shirt
against the sleepy sun.
People say nothing is free,
nothing is pure,
nothing is perfect.
But they haven't had a day like this—
a free sandwich,
a new night,
and my silver linings girl.

New Favorite Things

Your socks in my laundry.
Following you home.
Hand hearts in rear view mirrors,
you bopping to the radio.
Little details in your drawings.
Tiny heat curls in your hair.
Feeling you breathe.
Hearing your heartbeat.
You in my t-shirts, sweatshirts, underwear.
Photoshoots and getting fancy.
Laughing, butts against your wall.
Your shoulder squeeze that calms me down.
Your scrambling smile.
Days at the mall.
Waking up in your bed.
You waking up in mine.
Hearing every day about your day.
Having so much more time.

ROLLERCOASTER

She is going to break up with me.
It's a combo of things.
The way you look down at the street
on the walk back from the show
and how your hand feels limp in mine.
You go upstairs ahead of me.
We sprawl out on your bed,
but you keep squirming
like you are having a nightmare.
You won't meet my eyes.
You say, "I don't know how to do this."
You say, "I've never had feelings like this.
So..."
I catch your gaze, hold it tight.
"You can tell me anything.
It's okay."
But it's not.
It's not,
my throat tells me,
closing up.
It's not,
My stomach tells me,
eating itself alive.
This is the last time
I will lay on this this bed.
The last time
I'll see you this close.
How much time
do I have left?
How much of you
can I memorize?
My hand flies to your cheek.

So warm.
I brace for cold.
Your eyes fill.
"It's okay," I say.
It's not.
It's not.
It's not.
You say, "I love you."

The Strangest Thing

The strangest things make me think of you.
A group of men jump off the diving board like kids.
It's fifty-five degrees out.
One of them yells,
"Rate my pencil dive!
I'm gonna touch the bottom!"
The cool concrete shocks my feet.
I swear I see you next to me
in my reflection in the water.

A woman screams for her lost pet—
"Barker" or maybe "Archer,"
grasping the sculpture garden's fence like she is trapped inside.
She's back again the next night, two blocks over.
I want to scream too, for Barker or Archer to please come home.
And, for you.

My mile-long bike ride takes an hour
as I watch the solo kayaker until the last ripple dissipates,
because I don't want to leave
the feeling of you.

You used to pause the scene when two girls kissed on TV.
I used to look away
and have to rewind till I could handle the way
my heart pushed against my ribcage.
The way my eyes burned.
I'd think, no one is supposed to feel this much.

But the strangest thing is,
when I look at you, I feel all that and more,
and I don't look away.

You've shown me how to hold your
and the world's
gaze.

My Color

You play "Shade of Yellow" on our road trip to Houston
and say it reminds you of us
in my room
on early Saturday mornings.
My mom used to say yellow wasn't my color,
so I never wore it,
but now I sling my yellow backpack
over the yellow sweatshirt with the frayed cuffs
that I borrowed from you.
No one wanted me to love you.
Sometimes that's the best part.
It's all ours,
like those first pale yellow rays on a Saturday morning
before anyone else wakes up.

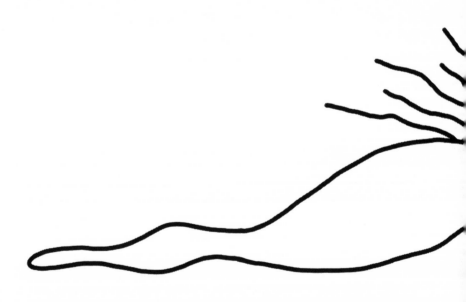

PERFECT MORNING

you
curled up
arms tucked into the neckline of your shirt
well, my shirt
at this point all your shirts are mine
your back glows in early light
you never close your shades
one curl falls over your cheek
you breathe
everybody breathes
but not like
you

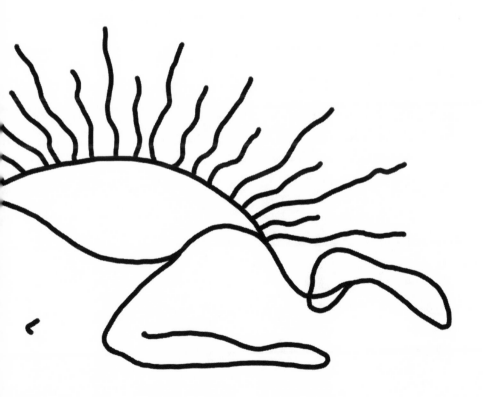

TINY GLASS BIRDS

You wanted to get a gift for my grandmother,
so we wandered the shop down the street,
chose a tiny glass statue of a bird.
"What's the occasion?" the checkout girl asked.
I said, "Meeting the grandparents,"
and you laughed.
She smiled a non-customer-service smile
and said, "Good luck."
The air felt fresh and perfect,
showing you around the yard I ran circles in
as a little kid.
The fence I ripped my dress on.
My favorite climbing branches.
It smelled mossy, the way it always did.
But when we went inside my grandparents' house,
I felt it:
Them, older.
Me, older.
All of us, different.
I missed them, though they were right there,
tossing salmon salad.
I couldn't remember what I used to say,
sitting here at this same table
all those times,
all those years away.
I missed me, though I was right there.
I told you that,
lights off in the guest room
right before we fell asleep.
The next morning,
my grandmother had you put the little glass bird
in her tall glass case,

next to the other one
I hadn't remembered
I'd gotten her before.
My chest ached the whole three hours home,
the sad-happy way,
one hand on the wheel,
one hand in yours.

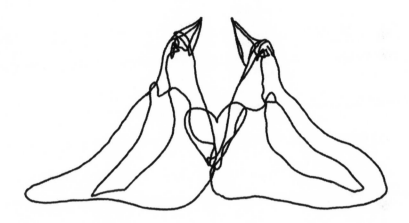

SHE'S HOME

The nights I waited for you,
I sat on my floor in your Aces T-shirt
that didn't smell like you anymore
and tried to read,
but you were more interesting.
You eating teacakes off a tower tray in rainy-grey London.
You in New York City, turning street corners in shiny new boots,
sipping an espresso martini.
You on a quiet Jersey block, feeling 16 again
in the worst and best ways.
I could see you, I swear I could,
but slowly, your edges blurred,
each day further
from the truth.
How could I tell
what was a story of my swirling mind,
and what was really you?
You started to seem impossible
until one hard knock, unlock,
you,
here and real, warm, solid, soft.
She's home, I thought.
She IS home.
Lovelier than any story
I could dream up.

CHOICES

There's the first date,
first kiss,
first "I love you,"
your eyes glassy,
because you couldn't find the words.

There's the first time I met your parents,
how my hands shook
asking your mom if she needed help in the kitchen
while you were in the shower.

And the first time you met mine,
diving for the ball
playing tennis against my dad.

Now you say
you might be transferred.
We might have to
make a choice.
You tell me about
       program differences,
       moving trucks,
       costs of livings,
eyes glassy again.
All I hear is
        we
            and
                choice—
The first time I've heard them in the same sentence,
the first time I know for sure—
    we have chosen
        each other.

Photos at Your Parents' House

You had a converse-shaped cake for your ninth birthday.
In kindergarten, you dressed up as the kid from *Motorcrossed*
and insisted your mom give you two braids under your helmet.
You were always holding onto your older brother,
even though he never let you find any Easter eggs.
You got a fedora on your road trip down the California coast
and wore it all through seventh grade.
You were once on the Mets fan cam,
and when you played catcher on your fourth-grade softball team,
the pitches would bruise your hand,
but you were too scared to tell your coach.
You had your same dimples
and button nose
and expressive green eyes
that looked a little sadder
around when you turned thirteen.

I heard once that if you talk to someone about a memory
in enough detail,
when you think of that memory,
you will feel them in it with you.

So tell me:
What did it taste like?
What did your class say?
How did it feel on your head?
Look at you, superstar.
Give me your hand.
That looks rough, my love.
Let's ice it when we get home.
You're the strongest girl I know,
and I love that you are different.

It will all make sense someday.

When I said I wanted you,
I meant every single you
in every single moment.

New Orleans

Last time, I was here with a girl
who looked both ways
before taking my hand.
You spin me around
to the sounds of the street band.
Dip me.
Kiss me.
We make this place
new.

In the Car

I love the way you sing along
to songs you've never heard.
It's how you love, too—
when the music is right,
you don't even need
to know the words.

QUIET

You,
making toast in my kitchen—
our kitchen.
When will it sink in
that you live here now?
You take your coffee out to the balcony,
leave your phone here on the counter,
so it's just you
and that mangled tree,
the city skyline,
early light.
I watch through the window
and marvel at
how good you are at silence.
When you come inside,
I am playing piano.
You step around the boxes
and go to wash your mug—
your mug
in my kitchen—
our kitchen!
I get up
and hug you from behind,
rest my head on your back.
I love you, I think but don't say.
I hope this never sinks in.
I know that you can feel it.

THE ANSWER (MAYBE V)

There are infinite kinds of love,
and you are meant
for every kind
you dream of.

REBECCA BENDHEIM writes books, poetry, and too many text messages in a row. She earned her B.S. from Vanderbilt University and her MFA in Writing for Children and Young Adults from the Vermont College of Fine Arts. She types poems with the nationally-renowned Typewriter Rodeo poetry troupe, teaches middle school English, and records weekly radio poems for Texas NPR. Rebecca lives in Austin with her girlfriend and their spirited orange cat. More at www.rebeccabendheim.com

SARAH ROSA GLICKMAN is an artist living and working in Durham, NC. Her art is deeply rooted in celebrating both the simplicity and complexity of being human. She focuses on the power of distinct lines and bold color in her constantly evolving exploration of emotion, nature, and just what it means to be alive. She hopes her work empowers others with the same strength and perspective it gives her. More at www.artbysrg.com

ACKNOWLEDGEMENTS

A million thank yous to all my COMING OUT PARTY planners, party-starters, and those who comforted me when I was crying in the bathroom.

First, the team at Burlwood Books—Sarah Beach, for your encouragement, patience, and meticulous edits. I can make an em dash now (see above)! Andrea Wofford, for the gorgeous cover. I could stare at the front of this book forever. And most of all, Sean Petrie. Thank you for believing in my work and for being with me on this book journey. When I feel stuck, you are here with a mason jar and a typewriter, asking what my biggest writing dream is. So many have become reality, and I know we will make more come true together and have an awesome time doing it.

To my family—I am the luckiest daughter and older sister in the world. Thank you for loving me unconditionally. Thank you for acting in and/or watching the many "productions" I wrote and directed as a kid, and somehow always finding something complimentary to say. I am a writer because of you all.

To my writing community—my VCFA advisors An Na, Jenny Ziegler, Linda Urban, and Corey Ann Haydu; my fierce VCFA class, the Line Tamers; my agent Patricia Nelson; and the friends who have convinced me to keep going time and time again, Erin Baldwin, Stefanie Hohl, Max Bronson, Courtney Cloutier, and Ruby Baker. You have shown me how to find the heart of my story and how to write seriously enough to pull it out and onto the page.

To my friends—thank you for all the love, support, and silliness you bring into my life. Especially you, Sarah. Getting to grow up together is one of my greatest joys. Getting to experience your beautiful art is another. From *The Eric and Gabe Show* to this book, I know this isn't the last strange and life-affirming project we will take on together. The way you see and question the world has always inspired me, and I am so proud of where it has taken you.

To my first readers—Chloe Lawrence, Allie Verrilli, Sean Petrie, Kari Anne Holt, and Julia Bendheim. We all need that first small "yes!" that makes it feel possible. Thank you for being mine.

To all the girls I've loved and liked before—thank you for giving me content for this book.

To Benji—thank you for sitting on my computer when I needed a break.

To Allie—thank you for loving, bribing, and dancing me through this book. I love you.

To my younger self—thank you for each of the 30+ journals you have filled on the quest to unravel your heart. It'll be worth it.

—Rebecca

Cover design by Andrea Wofford

Front cover photo by Sean Petrie

Back cover art by Sarah Rosa Glickman

Interior typeset in Adobe Gil Sans and Garamond

Cover typeset in Adobe LFT Etica and Barlow Condensed

BURLWOOD BOOKS

Burlwood Books is a small,
independent press in Austin, Texas.
We are dedicated to art that celebrates
the messy, vibrant, mistake-filled
wonder of life.

www.BurlwoodBooks.com